for Finbar
and all the little Furies

Acknowledgments are due to the editors of the following where some of these poems have appeared:

Abridged; *Agenda – Broadsheet 3*; *Borderlands –Texas Poetry Review*; *Electric Acorn*; *Drogheda Writes*, (Ed. Roger Hudson & Maggie Pinder, 2007); *Garm Lu* (St Michael's College, Univ. Of Toronto); *nthposition.com*; *Portrait*; *Revival*; *Riposte*; *The SHOp*; *Sentinel Poetry*; *Southword*.

The Garden of Earthly Delights was first broadcast on RTE Radio One's *The Poetry Programme*, February 2007.

Thanks to: Noel King, editor, Doghouse Books; Drogheda Bright Sparks reading series; Drogheda Creative Writer's Group; Louth Create Arts Fund; OUSA FC Conferences; Anna O'Byrne; Poetry Ireland/ Éigse Éireann, Todd Swift.

Contents

Quis custodiet ipsos custodes

Listen, said He, *You take the core*
if you want; just leave me the crust.

So, we learned to break sunlight,
a composite cataract of colour;
discovered gaps between them
and burst the locks of starlight:
all that we would know of age.

Now, we soar beyond sound
singing past white noise,
violating gravity's fall to
peer at Diana's sullied rock.

We are but blood and bone,
expansion still governs us:
can we know this universe,
side to side, top to bottom?

Time has us caught like flies;
amusing experiment played out.
Are we but a stone's throw
from the ominous art of distraction?

Quis custodiet ipsos custodes – Who watches the watchers

Roosters

My granny used to soak the spuds too,
making it easy to peel them later.
Part of morning's ritual was topping
their pot with water. Later, after
fowl were fed and *tae* and bread were ate,
she'd peel them slowly, humming all the while
a medley of *Moore's Almanac* songs.

Steeping my potatoes now, as she did,
brings her *Four Green Fields* down the years to me.
Scaly and red, these Roosters, instead of
her soft Queens; mine tattle of modern machinery;
long scars that I smooth away with a stainless
peeler. I split them with a long, broad knife,
rinse them down and leave them by for dinner.

SOS

We write code for here
and now. *Emoticons*
replace strained faces.

Whatever happened to
da, da, da, dit, dit, dit –
that old binary combo,
that old black magic?

Was life simpler then,
more real? Virtually,
I'm all for diversity,

I just don't want to
lose the creases of you,
the scent and taste
of valid, sticky, existing.

The State of That
or Feminist Literary Theory

Sandra and Susan took the madwoman
from the attic placing her in full view.

Dirty, dishevelled and cold,
like an ungrateful child
she burnt the house down
in protest.

She wasn't insane.
She just needed a leaf
from Medea's book —

better a burnt offering
than a dead one?

A Domestic Campaign

I - The Struggle for Supremacy
as told by Sister Anne

My greatest kitchen rival
is the thinnest veil of grease,
her droplets coalescing
in crooked cracks and corners.
Her tacky coat on all my delft
embellished with her comrade
dust, she takes the glamour off.

II - Ethnic Cleansing
as told by Sister Joan

Daily washes I peg out,
reform heaped on kitchen chairs
isolated from the soiled
in relation to the floor.
A linen basket crusade
that humble lather doth pursue;
stalemate, without giving ground.

III - Ousted by Usurpers
as told by Sister Ursula

The offspring in their burrows,
one more affray? Or should they
be let hold onto their reigns?
Here a hidden bower, there
an encampment, elder free.
Their vast territory mapped –
crayon scribbles on the wall.

IV - The Enemy Within
as told by Sister Gisella

Adversary, nuisance dust,
for worse (or best) in winter.
Amassing an unseen hoard
her drifts pile upon the floors.
Its multiplication flouts
my best efforts and sighing
I sweep. I must always sweep.

V - The War on Want
as told by Sister Martha

Bubbling in the large stockpot,
surplus from a Sunday meal.
Cut, weighed and calculated,
huddled on a warm platter
over potatoes steaming.
Drawn and quartered to their side,
carrots swelter in the heat.

VI - A Messy Mêlée
as told by Sister Helen

The shire-ware's lacklustre;
household scum of skin, ruined
foams congeal, compounded by
surrounding shaving speckles
that other hands sluiced – missed.
Ugh! I spray my wonder-goo,
with velvet-iron-glove I scrub.

IV - Skirmish With a Hoe

as told by Sister Isidore

Gardening, what a title! –
Seems a conflict betwixt wild
and tender domestic types.
More oftentimes than not the
cunning weed prevails the way.
Without my wearied rout, what
chance my prized summer blooms?

Christmas Eve, 1974

Satsuma scent and Old Spice
set off jingling bells in my head;
Spruce pine baubled with
shiny blues, reds and golds;
tinsel fronds that furl through
every twisting, uneven branch;
tinfoil star hoisted and
attached to the topmast.

I am forever seven
in that photograph,
polo-necked and trousered,
with much brushed hair.
I proffer my gift forward
like an Eastern princeling,
smiling on Christmas Eve.

Tír Tairnigiri

a land of promise, or the married state

The daughter of the sea
and the son of man
went oar in hand
past the breadth of land.

They picked out
a white rock, a black rock
and held a courtship
with gifts of fish and stone.

But she wanted water
and he his land.
They made their peace
between the seaweed edge
and the kelp bed.

Sang Réal

Take one winter's day sliding sunset,
chop finely and brown in a large stockpot.
Add onions halved and sliced
and salty tang of tears drawn involuntarily.
Season with a smattering
of children chattering
about Halloween costumes
and add water.
Bring to the boil and simmer gently
on the stove of your soul.
Serve with a portion of nostalgia and
garnish with relatives.
Serves twelve.

Sang Réal – literally, blood royal

Namesake

Song for Sinéad

Through winter softness mild
I cozied your weight within,
waiting for this new production.

My heaviness grew that spring,
your life quickening in my bulge;
I removed your father's ring.

The birth day arrived like others;
the gorge-deep gouging as
you were pushed into life's passage.

Finally you burst out –
furious at your eviction;
I marvelled at your newness
and named you for
Crazy Jane.

Jesus!

was crucified
in my back garden.
I know! I've seen the
tall wooden cross withered
by sun, rain and age – and
the lines they stuck in
to feed him juice
when he was dying.

I forgive 'em,
He cried,
for all their sins
I've died. I took it on
myself to do this in memory
of you all.

No-one ever *heard* that
conversation.
But the pylon remains;
steel or wood – there it is
without complaint.

Death of the Innocent

Their sun-strewn bedroom hazed
with the scent of exhaled alcohol,
tiny dust motes spiralled, caught
in the slanting draught of sunlight.

Grandma was gone to early mass.
I had gone into their room
in search of breakfast; a small child
lively and artless in large volume.

Grandad huddled in the many layered
marital bed. Above the brown-barred
bedstead, a picture stood to:
Edwardian starch, patricians
ceding triumph to the future.

Grandma returned, suited and gloved.
I told her: *Grandad won't wake up!*

Her eyes snapped shut like tomb slabs,
her face curious in its closedness.
Here, she said, *have a bowl of Rice Krispies.*

What sound does bad news make?
The heavy tock of the mantel clock,
or the faint popping of toasted rice in milk?

Family Portrait

The Devil can cite scripture for his purpose.
                The Merchant of Venice, I. iii.

Pater, you were an only child.
Blessing thrown late into
long lassoed lives. With hands
you learned to make what shapes
your head would not hold.
                You grew.

When your bonny flock began,
you did what men did,
with fists and thrift provided
what little jewels could be
wrested from education.
                Did you forget?

Funny then, how lives turn round.
Blessings thrown on desert ground
have grown indeed, but they
turned to the light. Some now bear
your family name, but not
                your livid shame.

Famous Nude by Picasso

Today, I point two firm melons
at you. You latch on, voraciously,
pike baited.
                Later, I let you begin,
fine-tuning looking for your
favourite signal coming through.

But then, wanton takes over,
turns us about, directs things awhile –
furious porphyry almost wholly
out of grasp.

Then we go home
and have a nice cup of tea.

* porphyry – reddish-purple rock

Messalina's Challenge

Eyes flutter open. Sucking in her first
day breath of scent, wine-laden with last night.

A pungent odour of lukewarm musk sweat
couples with an overwhelming she-scent.

Her fingers traverse the body lying
next to hers; a light ruffle of chest hair

extends north and south to his covered loins.
Her fingers pulse with a flowing warmth now.

He stirs, his breathing deeper, turning
towards her as his eyes wide open.

She smiles at her command of impulse,
rousing to the babble of words outside

and hears the name *Scylla* slicing through
her bedroom window like a scything breeze.

She mounts her present consort, smiling:
I'm still not satisfied, nor sore, nor beat!

Poker Face

Here we are
back at the beginning.
We sip and talk
genialities.
And then...

...sharks fin
glides neatly
beneath the rim of alcohol.
Denies ever he was there
dares me to define,
                    despise,
                          or ignore.

Shall we deal in words,
you and I?
I will cut
        the
            deck
                three times.
You will deal the charms
at arms length.

Soon
we shall fall,
tumbling through
a pillowed future;
back set against the past.
You shall see my hand
and I shall watch your downfall.

The Garden of Earthly Delights

In the kitchen, Valentine,
it will begin with the green
curlicues of garlic shoots hid
in the cold shelf of the fridge.

The prying, bulging eyes of spuds
will wink in the clammy closeness
of their plastic bag. All being pulled
spring-tight tonight, through the tilting

built into their bolting seed husks.
And you too will respond with the flick
in your loins, the click in your head
as my hands riot in the radishes,

tease out the aubergine chunks,
toss together pillows of cherry tomatoes
and delight in these firm ruins
of last year's seedpods. There,

Valentine, is where you will begin.

Watery Prophecy

A greased crystal ball
is my kettle, pressed into service
for soothing cups of tea.
I keep its insides clean,
its purity hidden within,
through the ritual
of everyday living.

Your leaves please,
at least those you have not slurped.
Turned over, the ceramic
cup scrapes on saucer white.
You have seen much sorrow.
Who hasn't?
But, your luck is about to change.

Emergence

As the focus shifts onscreen,
layers of fat and bladder give
way to an image; teeth buds, skull,
arms and hands. A curlicue spine
all turned out from one fertilized
nucleus; one zygote.

And the focus shifts.
The factory needed workers.
They came in droves, with
builders and roofers all tumbling after.
No call was made; they just came.
The suburbs rose from
one side street, one city.

Another slide show shows
the glass house exposed.
Its inhabitants have been
here fifteen years, watched
by a greater being. Their queen
laid a future
that emerged howling
into the man-made storm
of tomorrow's world.

So, we prod that mass,
manipulate the medium;
watch flora atrophy from
the empty vessel's fulcrum.
We share a future grown
by mould, fledged onscreen;
reduced to zero and one
and all the fractions
in between.

Sea Circlet

three fishers went sailing away to the west,
Away to the west as the sun went down.
Charles Kingsley

I sent a rolling, clinging mist
to deceive, devouring your landscape,
scouring your steps, winking out
the starlight entombed awhile in water.
I sent dark red dust clouds
to silt up every open orifice
with silicates of sand, wearing
away your patience, curbing your steps.

I drone on in the cracks and stacks,
shifting lightly my viscous, sticky hold.
I will harry you, down all your days.
Even as you sit upon your bedrock, serene
while your faith juts westward,
still you turn to worship East
paying no mind to the Magi
screeching, pointing towards the oceans.

August Harvest

the wages of sin is death

An August day blistered
in latent asphalt heat.
Sister and I messing
in the back of a parked car,
our mother in the butcher's
across the street.

The car shudders,
a low booming rumble.
Mother sees
the shop window flexing
inwards, the soldier
stumbling, clutching his red
neckerchief and crumpling.

I see the tractor deflate
like the letting of air
from a space hopper.

Mother comes back,
revs up the engine
and leaves the square.

Sharp Ground Frost

The moon lies broken
as smatters of glass beside
the tin can hulk of a car.

It's cold, bone cold as I
scrunch across the courtyard
of memories, cauled

in a reflecting pool.
Glass glints catch the eyes'
peripheries. This is no place

for a snail's trail gone cold.
Safety has fled into the smear
of moonshadow. Blow cold,

East wind in the neap of spring;
tide to the imperfect puddle
of remembrance.

Alighting on Legends and Myths

Luchtar, Goibhniu and Credné Cred were three brothers involved in the making of weapons for the Fianna. I have co-opted their names in fashioning a fictionalised version of their mythology: their triune I have come to regard in much the same way as a male poet might contemplate his female muse.

In creating their stories, especially Credné Cred and Luchtar, I have drawn from Celtic and Nordic myth, conflating primordial archetypes, legends and imagined happenings. I confess to borrowing heavily from Tolkien's earlier work as edited by his son, Christopher Tolkien, as well as the Táin but must add that each generation of storyteller will always put their own gloss on their stories. I am not attempting to recreate 'saga' as our forebears have done: modern language is by its very use a process of glossing and evolution.

Legends and myths have a way of resurfacing in different cultures: names vary, details vary but the essences of these archetypes: supermen, gods and goddesses, remain the same. The fusing of modern language with what has gone before is a whole other study by linguists and provides both etymologists and Jungian psychologists alike with much to analyse.

We have another past besides the past that history tells us about, a past which is in us, in individuals, more livingly than the recorded past.

Colum, P. (2002 [1922])."Introduction".
Complete Fairy Tales (Grimm). London: Routledge.

Standing Stone

Cuchullain's eyes saw only war;
his mistresses: blood and death.
Blind was he to the charms of youth;
his own youth founded in gore-lust.

Here stands the fairest Findbhair,
a daughter of Scorn and Scathe
sent to appease or to recompense Ferdia,
a trick in the pale morning light.

For her mother's ruse and her trouble
she was cursed by luck to be set
ageless to the wheel of the skies,
heedless beyond the world's ken.

Luchtar's Song – of Weapons and Wood
(how Cuchullain's Spear came to be)

When tangled trees swept in girth
Across the fair flanks of Mistress Earth,
When stars ebbed in Eastern skies
And hastened hedgerows to charmèd song,

When the scent of loam was dank and new
And spring sap surged to herald growth,
Luchtar, wood-wizened, stood at ease
In congress with birch, rowan and ash.

Mused he:
Long have I served this wizened maze
Where trees are repository of the age,
My mind a likeness of the ways of wood;
A skein of brush caught by winds,
Both wended and withied by time itself,
How deep the reach of the forest.

I have surveyed the eldest boughs of trees
From sapling, stretch their way through years,
Envisaged me the straightest spears
From heartwood bole matured within;
I have picked from hazel, yew and ash
And worked their honest, pliant wood,

To craft the surest breadth and aim
Of seasoned shaft scorched by war;
But you, widow-maker, a challenge rise
With your willowed, crooked, twisting ways;
A spear by wayward cunning devised
Such as Scáthach's hound might firmly grasp.

II

Now, Ogma's trefoil gift did cede
Order to the weft of natures tapestry:
In dawn's first glint through dew drop seen,
He hung upon the spokes of the Eldar tree;

The bonds of the word-noose twisted in twine
Burst and loosed his life-draught forth
And coursed through Odin's wood well
Of deep-rooted memory, left to still.

The mirrored surface drawing all
To lie in charged dormancy awhile,
Sent the oldest of trees burgeoning forth
Till ever there was the tallest swathe.

Ensnared by Time's bewitching veil,
Ogma's spell-font spared no branch;
Luchtar remembers as he fists his hand
When dark Chaos ruled the ancient land:

Said Luchtar,
'Twas not for naught my kinsman hanged,
His source let seep into Earth's deep pool,
I have tended long your marshèd copse
And coppiced when the Seasons waned,
Waiting for the staunchest shaft
That I would know by setting sun:

Salix Tortuosa with its bark aflame,
Its spiralling and twisted stems,
Contorted leaves, convolvèd veins;
Bitter must have been your lineage,
Roots buried deep in Ogma's enigma –
Now, a champion's cause shall you exalt:

For I shall take you into these hands
And craft you with a subtle might,
You shall chain man's oldest song
To wars sought in the name of right;
For the hymn of blood in men's veins
Beats time with the lust of what it claims.

III

Hence the woodland hills stood ablaze
In the baleful light of that fair evening
As Luchtar took into his gnarled hands
The fevered willow-wand he craved.

He crafted from his tangled mind,
The wood gave bent to his thoughts;
A hollowed thread inside he bored,
Too small to see with untutored eye.

Detailed charms carved he with guile
In the crook of every hollowed curve:
The sign for protection of the aiming skill,
The legend for the whorling path of kill.

He burnished Salix with his secret lore
Prepared of beeswax and herbal blend;
At length the shaft was turned and satisfied
Luchtar grimly smiled, and poised it across his palm:

Now to scorch you in the fires of Dúin
To harden resined eternity.
The man who grips you may well be felled;
But destined to remain untamed,
You will outlast the bravest men,
For Luchtar's lore is older than the trees.

Within you have I set my riddled essence;
The proud might of aged heartwood,
The claim of vengeance in you set,
And whence from now a settling of scores;
Yours will be the bidding of the better man –
For yours will be the hero's feat.

The Wayland Feast

When holy scribes kneel down to pray
And bid the sun be on its way,
The stars awake at end of day
And command my feet to Goibhniu's hall;
In darkened mound beneath the ground
Red Goibhniu sits, of old renowned,
And evening lengthens as is its course
As mead is served as sweet as gorse.

In twilight then, not night nor day,
Where jack-o-lanterns thread the way,
In half-light Searbhan plays
Inside the keep of Goibhniu's wall.
Came I at last to brooding gate
And fearing then that I was late
I beat upon the resounding door
As many souls have done before.

There, Goibhniu stood beneath old walls,
His eye of fire did I enthrall
And so I entered those sturdy halls
To feast the health of heathen Gods.
By great stone table, in cold stone chair
I took my place to eat my share,
A feast of venison, wild swan and boar
Such as I never had before.

Goibhniu's glass is raised in toast
To all of us and him the host
And now I fear my life is lost
In dwarrow-delve, by angels cursed:
His fey words convey a tithe –
Those who hear condemned to writhe
And weep, for forfeit be their souls;
Their hearts and minds so quickly sold.

Too late they learn, fake mortal men
With elfin hair and bloodied hem:
The souls of men are but small gems
That Goibhniu lusts to smite in gold.
In Eriu's hills, 'tis often said,
Great Goibhniu rises from his bed
To claim men's hearts and twist with glamour
Between his anvil and his hammer.

As thunderclouds are wont to gather
And lightening sparks blast the heather;
'Tis not nature's vengeance – rather
'Tis mighty Goibhniu working souls;
And these he sends clothèd forth
To seem to men crafts of worth
As Elder beauty – and how we yearn
That our blunted wits might learn.

But man might strive towards the day
When cunning artifice might play
A righteous part: to point a way
Towards the light that is more fair.
So, take this counsel won with grist:
When found abroad in faerie mists
Return you home and pay no heed –
The fabled gift of Goibhniu's mead!

The Desire of Credné's Heart

I

When starlight kindled in the heavens
And stayed the reign of ever-dark,
When Earthen kind were not yet fettered
By wordish cares beyond their mark,
When sky was but a crystal dome
To hold a sun so wondrous warm;
Here was Credné, masterwright,
Whose lock held fast the rooted stock.

In deeping coomb, 'neath bitter ice,
Brooding Credné sat musing wise,
How Craft might shape a new device
Of glacial rock and silver light.

Spake he:
I that smote the mountainside
And fiery brimstone fountain rised,
I that pooled the lake and
Forged the river's course to take,
I that set the stars above
In velvet skies to rove,
Will craft anew an orb of awe
The very Seasons will adore.

An oaken casket have I long hewn;
Set with jewelléd frost and strewn
With silvern hinges, hasp and lock,
Inlaid with spells and carven runes.
The casket holds my wishes true
An inner sphere bereft in want –
To this end I'll seek further counsel,
'Tis time our kinsfolk met again.

II

In Time when Gods still walked the plain
And fashioned all that lies therein,
Dark Credné did his people seek
And summoned them unto his keep.
A banquet such as ne'er before
Nor ever since and never more
The locksmith held 'neath hollow hills;
Of all that came they ate their fill.

A feast of meats on high table laid,
From beasts that no more stalk the plain;
Their bones are all that since remain
Found now by men in latter days.

The feast was held in chambrous halls,
Credné's finest treasures kept there;
Arboreal frescoes graced the walls,
Shook out their golden leaves most fair,
Bedecked in gems with fiery glow
That warmed the grot with fairest blush;
All guests wondered, in murmurs low
At Credné's craft, his precious touch.

To those beholding from afar,
This host met, as weft of dreams;
Brightly woven, brilliant stars –
These were eldest of fey beings:
Here was Dark Samhain *one eye*,
There, Brigit, *morning star of cold*,
Fair-browed Lugh, *belov'd of men*,
And Bilé, Cold Heart, *proudest Lord*.

III

Thus the roving troubadour was stirred
To give accounting through the years,
The gathered host listened with accord
To birdsong sweet and darker fears;
All Suibhne Geilt's wisp of dreams –
But turned he then to Credné's themes
And sang the master's deepest reveries,
A honeyed voice that soothed all.

He sang how Credné delved the sun
Fashioned from the gore of Samhain's eye;
And how the sparks from Bilé's forge
Were stars set by him unto the sky;
And sang he Brigit's birthing pangs,
How Credné caught them in the starry cusp
And made them diamond hard and clear
Speckling beaches with their dust.

Then of Samhain bitter sweet, sang he low
How Credné caught the deepest of his breath
And mixed with gemstones this cruel blow:
Thus was snow and sleet in ice set.
And last his voice soared in the hall
To tell how Lugh and Credné had contrived
To make a Lady from flower'd fall!
Laughs now Lugh, thinking on his magic bride.

IV

Suibhne Geilt ends now his great song,
As a spell the rousing notes ring on –
Mighty Samhain rumbles to his feet:

Credné keeps his company well,
But there is more than savouring meat
When feats of old does Suibhne tell;
Marry, we would all inquire
The meaning of this moot?

Credné's widening smile it deepens
As the hidden casket is revealed,
Through oaken panels run silver veins
Glistening as though tears were sealed,
Beneath its facing; though what it cloaks
Is nothingness, bereft of making,
On this lack Credné speaks and
To his wish gives he the undertaking:

O Highest of all hopes are we
Gathered in my keep this night,
And I your craft and aid do crave
To fill the void – no oversight –
Together will we frame anew
An orb that each of you may hold
Within your kingdoms, but 'tis true
A share of your glamour it will hold.

V

Hence all heard Credné's fervent want,
And pondered on their best aspect
Of knowledge that could be bent
To suit the treasure in their midst.
With every Season Credné spoke
And each one nodded their assent;
Within the coffer would they place
A flavour of their respective reigns.

Brigit, bright-heart, plants within her pain
That calls the budding spring to grow;
Lugh lays the calling of autumn's wane;
Dark brooding Samhain rests a frosty breath;
Bilé sets the restlessness of summer toil.
Credné stands, and places he the whisper
Of his forging craft within the casket's
Clasps and closes down the hasp.

Now the banquet resumes once more,
Wine poured a second time and raised in toast,
As the casket sparks to flame upon its bier
Credné speaks once more in reverent tones:

Now the time of waiting has begun
Betwixt silt and wash of winter sun,
For our art will be for night;
An orb of ghostly, silvered light.
The sift of all the seasons' gifts
Bestows from each its own sway:

Her brightness ever will seem cold,
Because of Samhain's cruel blow;
Her gleam will mense o'er her face,
Through Brigit's pain and Lugh's soft wane;
The heavens ever doomed to roam,
From within the breadth of Bilé's realms;
And Credné's gift; her birthing mark
That shines out softly in the dark.

VI

Ceaseless, Fairest, Daughter Moon was
Thus named, and set in heaven for the first.
How Crednés honoured guests gasped
And gazed upon her beauty in ascent.

And often since has man remembered
Some small spark of this great deed:
For every moon-filled winter night,
In warming tired and weary bones
by our great wood-filled crackling fires,
Yet may you seek a remnant rent
From Credné's casket blazed to ash.

Luonnotar's Thoughts

In the beginning was the word and the word was made flesh

John 1:1

When first I tripped along
the secret sound, I beached my
babbled words, cast slung-shot
into shallow water, without thought.
I paddled, seduced by sea song,
caught in the whirlpool of wordcraft.
I yearned to sink like stone,
to know the drowning sea of words.

I am sore, weary and travel-stained.
My trial by words has cost me sense,
yet I fear that my complaint
sinks gently like other shallow vessels,
lost in the storm-swept sea.

And now? I would not say I have
the mastery of words; rather have I
strived to swim their ebb and flow –
to take comfort in the deepened
swell, in the oldest of all oceans.

Luonnotar – creator goddess of the Finns, said to have emerged from the Oceans.

Debussy Trapping Notes from Nightingales

On the lines of a page Claude transposes
the collected melody. Some are remnants sounded
together from daily life, caught on horizontal lines.
His bars track on, right across the white page,
peppered with black bodied birds that sit tight,
caged on the wires. When they take flight
from the broad-spread hands at the piano, his skills
shape their timbre and shadow. He wreathes
sunlight, wind and rain within their soaring,
beyond that dead page.
                              And at the close,
those sleek bodies alight again, gripping
to the lines with their twig-like claws, eye beads
shining within the confines of the page;
roosting with the breves until the next time.

Alice's Boudoir

I watched you
at your dressing table
through the looking glass.

Your left hand lifted
the silver-handled brush
and you began to sing
as you brushed
down the years.

I longed to copy you,
look through your eyes.
Carefully you softly
brushed dark tresses,
coyly eyeing yourself
as dimlight encroached.

You only ever turned
your back on me once,
when you gently
placed the brush back
in the coffin at the
end of the bed.

Truth and Beauty

mostly riddles

If we did not exist,
there would be no room
for my Mirror to show,
thought Alice, older now.

Eighty year old Alice
sits and thinks; private
memories only hers.
Remembering Einstein
and Tagore; their faults —
their truth was only realized
through men.

And what of you and I?
said Alice gazing fondly
at the Mirror: *trapped time*
sits here like dust; caught spinning
in the sunlight, like these
interwoven concepts —
a collective future frozen
by Cousin Lewis.

Knitting Serpent

for Penelope

> Entranced, I used to watch your work
> stretch on clicking pins of steel.
> One day, you taught me how to hold
> the twist and make my own work grow.

She took the twine
into the darkened recesses,
wandering wildly

> But I was always dropping stitches
> that unfurled into gaping holes.
> Carefully you'd unpick my work,
> start me again and off I'd go.

from season to season;
looking back always,
to trace the twisted cord's progress.

> You made me make my own school jumpers.
> I came to hate July's dead heat
> knitting up the bargain yarns
> just in time for school's return.

There was no end, no beginning
to her searching, groping blindly
Jane saw all ways – but remained mute,

> Later, came complicated patterns:
> a cable, moss stitch or basket-weave.
> Your tricks taught, corrections made,
> my new repertoire outgrew yours.

tongue-tied in the web of fine twist.
Her fingers grasped,
still aching to reach the end,

> I yearned to stretch beyond your patterns
> faking up the antique designs,
> yet you insisted on *your* stitches
> knitted in the dullest twist.

the centre, the eye of calm.
There, only
the shattered symmetry,

      Long since, after you unravelled
      I still complicate time and stitch;
      no threadbare yarn, no knots entangled –
      tongue untied by wordy skein.

blood moon radiant,
fingers crooked behind.
There wasn't much left to see.

Extraction of a Smithy

An iron forge once stood beneath the playroom floor
in the heart of Clonalig, where once a smithy's anvil rang
hot metal under pound. The flicker of his measured
blows spark-skewed and he was caught in a life pulse
that winter's day:

The locks here, he murmured across the temporal plane, *open to
another set of keys. You'll have to learn the trick by taste.*

I spent years at books and learning, to understand
the ways of words and how they could tame men.
How my kin's blood twisted this tongue
around those keys and my mind learned
to forge a path from metal and become
a thoroughfare of thought.

I wonder did those craftsmen clear the mind
as they raised the hammer in servitude to song?

I desire to strike my name upon this page
as surely as those blows, and know this inscription
last a thousand years or more beyond the meaning
of words lost in the flow of lingual change.
But I am just another branch of the family of the smith,
doomed as all the others to be grounded into dust.

Song for Gwion Bach

Cross-legged, he leafs
through manuscripts, testing the names
of constellations on his noiseless tongue;
imagining a home-made observatory
from cardboard tubes sticky-taped together.

He has notions of seeing unknown stars
but a flipped, inverted view
of the moon is the best he can do;
an orange glow on tracing paper.

A birthday telescope opens a small crack;
the blue and yellow plastic tube wobbles,
its unsteady legs skewwhiff.
The faulty, fingerprinted lens limits
a lesser scope, the universe grease smudged,
stars still pinholes to the galaxy.

Later, a screwdriver allows him nuggets
inside his range. Dismembered mirrors,
tubes and levers, become solid things;
he palms them close to his screwed up eyes.

Gwion Bach – the Welsh counterpart to Fionn and the tale of the Salmon.

Mrs Mop Sings the Blues

Clear out the collected detritus of a full five years
and see how the change that visited me
has carved its own landscape across the walls of home.

Things that I no longer need, or those that went astray –
largely like the thoughts in my own mind.

I have domesticated and disciplined so long, that these drawers
are keen to observe their own de-fragmenting.
Today's clutter remains. It is merely reorganized.

The Covenant
after Leonard Cohen

*I do set my bow in the cloud, and it shall be for a token of a
covenant between me and the earth.*   Genesis 9:13

I am not Marianne
and this is not 'so long'.
It is the last day
of a good year.
The old sun has dared a shine.

A believer in portents
would say a blessing
has been served.
But I know signposts
are for reading,
omens for heeding.

And so a harvest glows between us two.
A flame that moves us both
as I hang upon your cruciform,
braced for this acceptance;

our covenant is given freely,
not said, nor signed, nor sealed.
It is the motion between
two, that transfigures each.

Torcs (and Other National Treasures)

Stored beneath a saturated mire,
the land had claimed
its cherished trésor
but yielded it to a pair
of greedy hands.

The torc was twisted then
by servitudal status. And now
coiled time seeps from that spring.
A narrow wrist wasted by
ancestral history waits
for another hand held fast –
stayed against the pressing
of fresh firm flesh.

I would pan for other gold,
leathered skin, an untold story
encased within the soft tanned frame.

Teach Duin
a divided house of holding – Skelligs

Did they come to their rock,
Maighdean-mhara, to be wedded to yours,
bonded by the fate of the crossing?

The elder ones would watch
the younger struggle with interest:
Here comes another who has
not loosed the bonds of 'stock and stone'.
He will learn.
They nodded their assent as the heads hoved,
scaling Jacob's stairway, shouldering parcels
like a betrothal of guilt.

And you, *Maighdean-mhara*, watched detached;
sun basking on your glistening galleries,
the foppery of men – tide to their rock.
The seasons washed you by, then the seasons withered.

Expectant you waited; they fixed stars
in the firmament, saw the ebb and flow
as the crux. You notched the rock,
kept account – God's ledger.

Now the stench of your filial friends
long since fled scourges your mind;
transfixed in the present,
chained to your rock, in counterpoint
to theirs.

Maighdean-mhara – sea maiden
Teach Duin – tech Donn – the gathering place of the dead, said
to be an island lying to the south-west of Ireland, presided over by
Donn, God of the dead.

To The Naturalist

The Three Billy Goats Gruff

Who is he,
the gnarled troll
who lurks under
the bridge?

His tightened stranglehold
on nature's noose of
putrefaction and decay;
its preserves were once
his reserve.

A subtle arrogance that stole
through the poet's brave rhythms
rounded and bound the trave.
Suibhne Geilt has informed
the crafty traveller.

And I must trip-trap lightly
through his word-snare;
the littlest Billy Goat of all
may cross to taste
the sweetest grass
that lies beyond the bridge.

Suibhne Geilt:
Sweeney — a king cursed by St Ronan (Christian gloss) so that, in
spite of his human form, he assumed the characteristics of a bird,
leaping from tree to tree.
Geilt — one who goes mad with terror from the field of battle.

Radio Hams

Tonight just doesn't make sense;
I have tried to listen carefully
to mangled truths. I'm tuning in

to my own warped wavelength
once again. You have tried too;
patience with an untried phrase –
a dead-reckoning is what you prefer.

We are tired now of trying and
so the conversation begins
for real. I tell you moribund tales
and you laugh: *That can never be*

as long as you are here with me.
Still, I am unconvinced by darkness
and the smell of summer turning
in the wake of our betrothal.

Trench Monument

It wasn't the flies so much as the reek
caught downwind that giddied passers by.

The lush green of new moulted shoots
smoothed the vale down to the river.

Behind, a stand of pines on the crown of the hill.
The buzzing becomes an engine purring

closer towards the hill crest.
Carcass caverns loom stark, lying

as they had done in November permafrost.
But now, in spring, white maggots blindly creep

from thawing flesh remnants, writhing, vying
for their own stale warmth, feeding the biomass,

reducing the remains to a future fossil.
Particles of dust, carbon atoms:

emissions in a shell-shocked future.

Mikey and Trisha

a man's subjugate creation
                              J.R.R. Tolkien

His hammer tips and taps,
cut with timber sawn refrain,
falling off-cuts clatter, pause –
then back to hammer raps.
He hews everyday frustration
into useless household gewgaws,
a demon's wish inside, suppressed.

A man of middle age might
settle on her best burnt offerings;
lukewarm leavings half-cooked.
How does he save grace or right,
when she crows on the midden
of a seedless garden, weed-choked?

Shopping Trolley

a 'no frills' shopping experience

The trolley that a man gave me
he had used to push around
his middle-aged contemplations
past the coffee and the tea
and toiletries.
He went for the TVs –
bargain of the week!

I used the trolley to push
my two and half years
of fuddled frustration,
concentrating on porridge
and packed lunches
with variety but no spice.

The trolley I gave in turn
to a tartan-wheelie-bag woman.
She zoomed in on it;
her basics to buy
with her weekly pension.

That trolley saved us all
from fumbling with
our spare change.

Retale

It is always threes in Wales,
where Rhiannon is stubborn
and direct. She saves female guile

for the bedroom or the birthing stool,
or shouldering her punishment
for the length of time it takes

to watch a child from nothing
to walking and talking sense;
more so – a son like Prydwedd

needs care; a little mind like that
needs feeding and watching, away
from his mother's tongue.

Where bitter words scourge like flails
from visitors and kin daily,
who knows when patience will deliver;

Rhiannon always keeps hope,
scanning for her cares to come back;
even as Pwyll watches her at the gate.

Samhain Reckoning

You were an old flame guttering,
sputtering with the lie of life.
Closer to extinction you lived,
armchair convictions condensed to
badge the sleeve of your hair shirt.

You imagined me a mirror
fit for moulding to your image.
But I proved more enigmatic
than Leonardo's lady, my length
cramping, hampered by your frame.

What did you see when the rattle
stuck fast, final, in your black craw
and then fluttered from your mute mouth?
A gilded moth trapped, flickering
in the swirling wake of summer skirt.

Nostalgic Blanket

Today is blanketed in grey velvet silence.
All are caught in this twilit hour
between death and life. The land itself
waits for the imperceptible turning of the year.

We dull our senses, overindulge our heathen
ancestors. A time for thought sunk deep
in armchairs before flickering images
cast forth from empty vessels.

We are caught in the cotton of waiting –
passing time hesitant in hoping;
springing on three months to
full awareness, where the muted notes of

passing cars will shriek again the rule of men.
I am the changeling, nose pressed to glass,
watching and heeding the timeless ways of men;
their cozening lives behind the lies.

Deathwishes

I want a filmy horizon of blue skies and clouds
visible from a mature, green, shady garden.
It should be summer – a long hot summer,
ponderous with bees that drowse
towards huge blowsy, drooping flowers, all reds and purples.
You should be there too.

In the evening when the long-legged
daddies come out to waltz,
we should dance too, holding
each other lightly but firmly.
We should laugh at stupid things.
And when it is over, we should sleep.

The Crumbs of a Prudent Housewife's Year

after Dylan Thomas
Being kept and re-used to make stuffing for the turkey!

When the thieving hands of time steal back
What the tilt of the seasons has lent,
When the dim twilit hour fades in our hearts
Insistent the chime of Old Chronos' song.

When the cook's thought turns to humble pie
And tender stewed meat and barley soups,
Then you know truly that winter is come
All toil of the year is the tale in the broth.

When the lacklustre light of dreary doom
Calls the blackened kettle to hale good cheer
'Tis then all good folk give greetings and say
You won't feel it now, 'til Christ's mass is near.

Do Mad People Have Mad Gardens?

Mary, Mary quite contrary,
how does your garden grow?
With thickets and trees,
thatches and reeds,
that's how her garden grows.

With homemade drains
and shale from Spain,
overgrown trees
and dead stumps with ferns,
with the rushing of water
and a binding road
and an old cesspit,
to keep all her shit –
that's how!

The Willow Pattern

The sodden marsh field
mourned long by the willow,
the reason for weeping forgotten.

Weaving in the tree branches
in a mean October breeze
hangs an old smock-dress,

so '70s flowers faded
brown like the bog grass.
And the weeping tree
shedding its leaves;
one by one.

Grace Notes for My Parents

If music be the food of love, play on
Give me excess of it, that, surfeiting,
The appetite may sicken and so die

Twelfth Night, I. i. 1-3

You're angry again:
I can tell – silence drips –
muzzled rain too disgusted
to fall whole.

I have learned to read
pitch perfect tones, scale arpeggios,
orchestral scores that strike chords
of nothing.

Misery oozes through
the breeze blocks of my bedroom.
Gazing at the blind ceiling
I wonder who offended who?

Now, frustrated rage filters
through; one voice raised –
the weeping other discrete
in its crescendo.

Resolution waits on
another night.

Barbara Smith (b. Dublin, 1967) grew up just over the border in South Armagh. She moved to the Republic at eighteen and was employed for a while as a tile artist in Dundalk. Like many in the early '90s she moved to the UK in search of better opportunities, which she found as a Press Reader with Romeike & Curtice, a press cutting agency in North London.

Her return to Ireland was prompted by the birth of her first child and she took up a position with Droichead Arts Centre, Drogheda. This allowed for more intense involvement with literature and the writing community and led to the publication of her chapbooks, *Gnosis*, (1996) and *Poetic Stage* (1998). In 2005, she was chosen for Poetry Ireland's / Éigse Éireann's Introductions Series.

Since then, Barbara has studied for a BA Hons. Literature, to be awarded this year (2007) and has been accepted into Queens University Belfast for a MA in Creative Writing (07-08). All of this Barbara combines with the financial and family demands of raising six children with her partner in the *Wee County*.

Barbara blogs at http://intendednot2b.blogspot.com/ and can also be found on MySpace and Facebook.

Also available from DOGHOUSE:

Heart of Kerry – an anthology of writing
from performers at Poet's Corner, Harty's Bar, Tralee 1992-2003
Song of the Midnight Fox - Eileen Sheehan
Loose Head & Other Stories - Tommy Frank O'Connor
Both Sides Now - Peter Keane
Shadows Bloom / Scáthanna Faoi Bhláth - haiku by John W. Sexton,
translations into Irish by Gabriel Rosenstock
FINGERPRINTS (On Canvas) - Karen O'Connor
Vortex - John W. Sexton
Apples In Winter - Liam Aungier
The Waiting Room - Margaret Galvin
I Met A Man... Gabriel Rosenstock
The DOGHOUSE book of Ballad Poems
The Moon's Daughter - Marion Moynihan
Whales Off The Coast Of My Bed - Margaret O'Shea
PULSE - Writings on Sliabh Luachra - Tommy Frank O'Connor
A Bone In My Throat - Catherine Ann Cullen
Morning At Mount Ring - Anatoly Kudryavitsky
Lifetimes - Folklore From Kerry
Planting A Mouth - Hugh O'Donnell

Every DOGHOUSE book costs €12, postage free, to anywhere in the
world (& other known planets). Cheques, Postal Orders (or any legal
method) payable to DOGHOUSE, also PAYPAL (www.paypal.com) to
doghousepaypal@eircom.net

*"Buy a full set of DOGHOUSE books, in time they will be
collectors' items"* - Gabriel Fitzmaurice, April 12, 2005.

DOGHOUSE
P.O. Box 312
Tralee GPO
Tralee
Co. Kerry
Ireland
tel + 353 6671 37547
email doghouse312@eircom.net   www.doghousebooks.ie